*Convalescence Dance*

*Also by Alexandra Sashe*

Antibodies

Alexandra Sashe

*Convalescence Dance*

Shearsman Books

First published in the United Kingdom in 2018 by
Shearsman Books
50 Westons Hill Drive
Emersons Green
BRISTOL
BS16 7DF

Shearsman Books Ltd Registered Office
30–31 St. James Place, Mangotsfield, Bristol BS16 9JB
*(this address not for correspondence)*

www.shearsman.com

ISBN 978-1-84861-550-2

Copyright © Alexandra Sashe, 2018.
The right of Alexandra Sashe to be identified as the author
of this work has been asserted by her in accordance with the
Copyrights, Designs and Patents Act of 1988.
All rights reserved.

Acknowledgements
Some of these have previously appeared in the following journals:
*Envoi, The Interpreter's House, Long Poem Magazine, Orbis,
Poetry Salzburg Review, Shearsman, Snow litrev,
Tears in the Fence, Time of Singing.*

# Contents

## Part I

| | |
|---|---|
| "a needless…" | 11 |
| a Tear | 12 |
| Lenten | 14 |
| Autumnal | 16 |
| St. Peter's second conversion | 18 |

*from* Confessions
    "When my eyes were lakeless…"    19
    "When my hair locks lay…"    20
    "When a daily boat…"    22

| | |
|---|---|
| "arid alluvial / wrong and vital…" | 23 |
| "Winter prevails, its mended shoulder…" | 24 |
| "Winter prevails / and kneels above us" | 25 |
| "Sadness prevails   with an anonymous" | 26 |
| "The month of thirst / and the Kings' journey…" | 27 |
| "Dividing meadows with a monastic short step…" | 28 |
| "No wind. The slowed down clock…" | 29 |

*from* Wandering cycles
    *"And eat our bread at the face of the window"*    30
    "a room insulated from time…"    33
    "Snow flakes and leaf-flakes…"    34
    "timber sleeps / fresh from birth"    36
    "To restore the outer edge of the table…"    38
    "If we stay untouched…"    40

| | |
|---|---|
| "The renewed kingdom…" | 42 |
| "arid alluvial / city stands out…" | 43 |
| Somnolence | 44 |
| Apocalypse eve (of the sinners) | 46 |
| Apocalypse eve (of the penitent) | 48 |
| Apocalypse eve (of the just) | 50 |

### *Alembics*

| | |
|---|---|
| 1. "It is water that drowns our faces…" | 54 |
| 2. "When the water subsides…" | 55 |
| 3. "It is water that waits…" | 56 |
| 4. "We thank ice" | 58 |
| 5. "Water speaks…" | 59 |
| 6. "The soliloquy of the water…" | 60 |
| 7. "Fire foreknows…" | 62 |
|    Interlude ( "Trees are called upon…" ) | 63 |
| 8. "Fire chooses the front door…" | 64 |
| 9. "Sunday: estuary" | 66 |

## Part II

| | |
|---|---|
| Spring Canticle | 69 |
| A Song for Elias | 70 |
| "If in the heart I find no water and no thirst…" | 71 |
| Epiphany | 73 |
| "A mine glass empty with water…" | 75 |
| "This tree departed from its species…" | 77 |
| "ink and paper  cross and…" | 79 |
| Mt. 5:39 | 81 |
| *from* Pastoral cycle: "Lime-painted trees" | 82 |
| *from* Pastoral cycle: "Substitute for the ink and paper" | 84 |
| Autumnal | 86 |
| Ode to Spring | 88 |

### *Fürbitte*

| | |
|---|---|
| "Offer fingerbones to the Lord…" | 91 |
| "Offer the Lord bloodless and dry…" | 92 |
| "Offer on the instalment plan…" | 93 |
| "Offer the Lord an ivory-green…" | 94 |
| "Offer the Lord  space…" | 96 |
| "Offer the Lord the bottomless nothing…" | 98 |
| "You are offered a rain…" | 100 |
| "You are offered a jasmine-scented …" | 101 |
| "You are offered a wing…" | 102 |

| | |
|---|---|
| Notes | 10 |

*á mon seul désir*

*Part* I

"We carry the brightness,
the pain, and the name"

—Paul Celan

a needless needed
stood at the door
a trace of salt
on her ring finger
she uttered a spell word
out of its home –
it stayed there, on her lips,
      bare,
      uttered,
overheard by the wind
of the staircase –
      she stood
seeing her eyes in their
      her
      silhouette
hoar-frosted over
windowpanes shutters
      needless
      ( needed )

## A Tear

And if I don't cry – where
do I look for it,
where
do my knees become one with the ground,
and crows cleave
into my speechless,
into the taut
cords of the violins

And if a tear holds fast
and saltless,
if
it presumes limpidity, and
if I obey the tear's presumption,

where do I look for my knees and the ground
in their orphan-like
separation

And still, should the knees
and the ground forgive me
and come
into their inheritance,
                              will I
be naked enough

to be crows and violins
and disinherit myself

from the tear ?

(And if the sea-salt and brine of the spoken
come to pass
through the millennial layers,
will they suffice
to enter the tear,

and will I suffice
for a single tear,

and will
this tear suffice ?)

## *Lenten*

And if the daylight
prevails in my vessel, and hands
are prevailed upon with the weight
of the scent
of mimosa and acquiescence,

I wake up in a clean month
with a monstrance space
in my chest.

Tear summons its secrecy, salt
imparts to the eye its saltness. A windless week
becomes a kingdom.

And if I confide in the fluid and simple
and measure with hours my calendar,

It is the penultimate day of completion.


Fruit lives by its juice
I taste on my knees
       and receive on my palm.

Its kernel sister to tear.

The looking glass pays out the years
stored overnight behind
    its amalgam.

           And if I confide in its golden
           warp and weft
           of skins and kernels,

the month of April knows
the value (qualified and added
by the thaw water) of

a tear.

## *Autumnal*

And if I stay still,
beyond the tear

at home with the leaf's
and the retina's
common   seasonal
need for abscission,
   with their secret
   reticulations,
   and their
   para-visual  stillness


And if the tear recalls
its name,
a monosyllabic
silence non silence,
beyond the hour
of the green, beyond
the arboreal and the *i*,


my hand will hear
the tear's echo
and hold in the hollow its humid
question

lipped by the leaf's wordless tokens, –
– lip-read by the years' empiric memory
stored within
the amalgam
  of the ocular


And if we remain
image- and speech-less
covered with eyelids, sunscripts and foliage,

no gust of time
would ever stir
our petiolate being.

## *St. Peter's second conversion*

Walk on water,
knee-deep in fear. The insomniac sea
has a host of centres, each
a hidden garden. Your walk is unrecognisable
from the fishing boats' vantage

your hearing and feet
embalmed in night.
The lighthouse belfry chimes you deeper,
the sand of somnolence dries off your shoulders.
You walk from water
to water. Pelagic beings are your
spouses,
are ford and island,
the pelagic voice has temperature of no-voice, –

no cock to crow.

## *from* 'Confessions'

When my eyes were lakeless
and my hearing seaweeds,
every word of ink
stood on edge
        and compelled
to brave the bridge
over the blank abyss.

When my hands were blind
and waitless,
every page took Pandora's risk;
        and a word freed from its ink
           swapped its liquid life for sap –
              with the trees.

In the lakeless and songless time
the blood and the sun
lived by full uneven circles:

the blank abyss was nourished with shadows,
with arid tumbleweeds
come from across
the years
    of quicksand.

*from* 'Confessions'



When my hair locks lay
        close to my mind,
and the comb knew by heart
its movements northwards,

and the conscious comb-like pace of the heart
was inaudible
outside the heart's chambers.

When the days struggled,
              counter-clockwise,
with the birds' itinerary of migration
across the pond,
with a wind shut in between the lungs,
with the fruits' itinerary
of decay.

When my eyes grew visions, arid and bell-less,
upon the towers. When my lips
were at home
with chimneys, attics and cellars,
when the doors grew like trees,
        and no windows could bear
a single fingerprint of the sun.

The years' sand overflowed the sand clock
and drowned its own
name and memory.
  And my season of birth was a season of thaw
  and burning forests.

*from* 'Confessions'


When a daily boat
        was our bread,
and a month – a fleet,
   a year – a navy,

we preached crusades to the birds of prey,
and our prey was the voiceless
birds of the garden.

When tightropes
were our wings,
we followed the straight line
parallel to the ground.
We unfolded sails
        against the wind,
and spoke water
and brine
        apart.

We sculpted wood into figureheads,
and stood for masts, and assigned
to our daily boats
        our own virtue. –

And counted
in separate units
knowledge, pain and time.

arid alluvial
wrong and vital, –

city and cradle


ring and noose
of the quays
  and the moon,

of suffocating inceptives,

of step-motherland arms
  open and vacant.


Seagulls weaned from water
prophesy a lake,
profess Februaries.


Vital, disowned,
stripped of the moorings,

  I am left on the right
  bank of the Ocean.

Winter prevails. Its mended shoulder
in the overcoat of endurance and clover.

naked cobbles
sadness' ancestry
refrain from the amplitude of their echoes.

Crows' indifference turns into mercy
within the lower
             atmosphere.
Voices are gone to encrow the South
                 led away by their voices.

The burning years of dust and orphancy
absolved and buried
in sackcloth and ashes.
Seeds sown
       preserved with frost.

Rooms are set towards the twilight
with ink and clocks and the static
deepening pages. The true hand is the rooms' cradle.
Yesterday's bread lost and found.

Winter prevails
               and kneels above us
with a long-held breath, and knees uncovered.
We adopt the unknown
ancestral years, and begin to collect
into its silent vessel
the snowflakes, come
from *Lisieux*, via the *Schauflergasse*,

      And eat our bread at the face of the window.


The aid is hidden and found
in the tear's
centripetal loving existence. Adopted,
our eye
is set aright
    within one and the same
    tear.

Lips are prevailed upon with the fruits
of our soundless winter garden. Behind their gates
we are delivered, – and kneel
above
    our selves,
clothed in the snow
of our naked winter.

Sadness prevails   with an anonymous
footfall across the courtyard,
the thread of undoing.
Candles and souls lit by the common dark
strip off and cast upon the wall
   the shadows   no longer
                     in common.

A crystalline composition of this inflamed dying
hour. The Waiting implodes and blows on its ashes.
Vigil
   is born, late and grown,
child and guardian. It
is
your crystalline gratitude. Your ever-happiness
kneeling down.

The month of thirst
and the Kings' journey
across our snow-
          camouflaged desert.

Our magnified leafless time
abridged by a walk:
across the courtyard.

The steam from the roofs hiding the star
shaping the thirty stars
          for coins.

   We observe the clocks
   elevated upon the towers
   and clasp our hands with forgiveness.

   The gates are closing and closing
   behind the pilgrims
   leaving and leaving our desert city.

Dividing the meadows with a monastic short step
                                          without a wake;
a snowed-under path between
the vine- and the grave-yard
                past *Würzburg*, a ladder of January.



With burnt hands carrying flames;
immaculate black,
                sackcloth and ashes in bloom –
                  the garment of soleness in unison with the wind.



carrying time across the bridge,
                across the estuary of Lethe.

No wind. The slowed-down clock may let go of its
straw- and tear-woven towers,
recover its breath. The north moves nowhere from the field
of vision and holds on with one fast finger
to the one sole promise
the towers left
in their wake.

They grow green, inaccessible to the upturned faces that
time now breathes out at long intervals. The space between
their sleep and wake disappears, and they are about
about to fly
to retrace their steps by way
of where the north
and the promise
lie.

*from* '*Wandering cycles*'

*1.*

*And eat our bread at the face of the window.*

Liquid tar covers our hands, the cold memory
takes wing. A butterfly each
patch of sunlight.
  We tune with silence our strings
  and lean against the wall
  our years' almanacs.
  Time's leafless archives are gone south,
         birdwise.
Symmetrical traces
of our elbows' fidelity
dwell on the tablecloth,
faithful to their
   patterns.


  Our hand lines
  conform to the warp and weft,
    and –
    coincide with the kingdom.


Leaning back we confide
in the chairs' uprightness and memory
  (tokens of their arboreal
  pre-existence).

They grow
    motionless, rootless,
with our arms for branches;
cushions, conversant with our texture,
keep the secret of our
    shoulders'
        configurations.


2.


The evening windowscape,
sunset and lampshade
blended within
the roomscape's reflection.

Bookshelves are
    parallel to the horizon:
fields and valleys
ploughed and lying fallow. –
Among the pages live sequestered
leaves and threads from the paths to the Garden.
    With our white-pure evenings
    we stencil the blank chapters.

Prophecies,
    read counter-clockwise,
yield to the fingertips' ( eyes' emissaries )
        auscultation.

3.


At twilight, our face
          of sublimated dust

dissolves – and coincides
with the face of the window.

    At dawn we start our walk
    over the safe bridges
       of our broken mirrors.

*from* 'Wandering cycles'

a room insulated from time, a daughter
of curtains, oblique light, clocks' perpetuated
and ever-deferred departure.

  leaves' soundless tokens
  breath yellowards,
      birds shed their voice
       in the September harbour.

Our room-fostered eyes
return home from the months of the harvest,
our hands bring seeds, the yield of the months,
offsprings of trees that
we have denied and had been.

Treefree, loosed from the cincturing bark,
we choose the chosen, and fill with water
anonymous cups
behind the window.

Leaves collect the summer voices, bare the birds,
attune with the clocks'
ever-perpetuation.

## from 'Wandering cycles'

1.

Snow flakes and leaf flakes'
alternating positions
   close and open
doors and windows,

measure the heart's itinerary
with the not-yet- and already-
   covered     un-covered
        distances.

*Helmutplatz 10*,
     a votive masonry,
sows a meta-lingual soil.
     Trees, liberated from human prefixes,
     encircle with their branches
     our de-verbalized being.

We grow with the trees, within each other,
shed the superfluous pairs
of hands, hemispheres, knees.

In passing,
autumnal clouds and birds
hail and impersonate our
ana-nominal species –
     ( in emulation of their passage,
       digits abscise from clocks ).

*2.*

An early morning, a timeless volume
of space and minutes, –
>        a deck set outside the over-
>        populated eventlessness.

The wooden planks cushion the sunlight,
one's hearing lies safe above the water.

( One walks into an early morning
  upon the ropes
  of one's own moorings. )

*from* 'Wandering cycles'

1.

timber sleeps
    fresh from birth.

we lend the woodcutter our hands,
veins of our
arboreal thought:

we clothe our shoulders with leaves'
stencil-precise reticulations.


2.

years' carpentering eye
carves into our purpose
venation and oxygen, –
a mute arboreal being is our
single task, –
we shed the speakable
through the abscission
of all the verbal.


Wood and fingers
exchange their rings,

                              their names are

intergraven:

in the interior silence,
we teach our hands to speak.




3.

we are shaped and become
our own
armrests and backs,
steads and drawers,

polished and covered with cloth
we abandon the need
for varnish and locks.

True to our raw material,
we remain inflammable,
heavy,
     floating.

Having learnt
     to correspond
to our structural immobility,
we are saved

and yield the Restorer
     our surface.

## from 'Wandering cycles'

To restore the outer edge of the table
forced into a faultful square –
to free its initial curve of the circle,
    chisel away the angle
    and save all without mercy.

The honey voice of the wood shavings
sings their last, uncovered purpose.
The smooth surface takes over,
along with us, disculpated,
absolved from being
furniture.

        The sunlight bakes us daily bread
        of nothing – leavened and salted
                with its recurrence.

        The wood shapes our common dwelling
        with its arboreal thought
        and a ring concept.

Walls embrace
our measure of space,
chairs grow backs,
        upright,
attuned with our conscience.

Time and bread cut in slices,
spread with awaiting,
sweetened per serving,
    we eat from empty porcelain plates.

Metamorphic and static, we slough
our off-white upholstery
and grow skin
    from the warp and weft
of: sunlight, nothing, partaking, tablecloth.

        ( From scripts and plants we collect
          our measure of oxygen. )

We inhabit the centre, the sole room,
its shelves and harbours,
valleys and fields:

    As our armchair
      develops the Ark's capacity,
        we are simplified,
          perfected,
            reduced
    to the bare fullness of being.

*from* 'Wandering cycles'

If we stay untouched
by windows and walls,

unleaned against
by backs and bolsters,

unrested under
by bed sheets –
  restful, uncovered by clothes,
  in our nudity, true and hidden. –

If we keep vigil,
counter-clockwise,
awake in sleep,
filled with the lamps'
          meek oily being,

 ( or if we descend the stairs' silence,
   kindled by light, dwelled
          from chamber to chamber.) –

If we stand still, sheltering roofs,
rained under, snowed under –
    with our hands collected in dew,
    our eyes absorbed in sunlight. –

We will exit the day
through the door of its eve,
effaced from the earth
by its own dimensions,
        and be delivered
                      from Language –
                      by Word –

perfecting into a single step
   our epistemological
choreography.

The renewed kingdom
deserts its gardens.
        It is a small walk,
    under the sun
recoiled into its zenith.
The path strews petals
to cover the paving stones'
soteriological configurations.

The obvious kingdom
embraces its source
with counterfeit lips,
counter-kneels, engenders its own accord.

The kingdom's halt is hidden in steps,
imprints of its heraldic mirrors
through which leaks
        at the kingdom's feet
the face it carried on its temples.

arid   alluvial   city
stands out
behind the syncopal
farewelling
solitude,

    boulevards restored
to their no-oneness:
with trees and knots,
    leaves and bows.

city sends out
its empty envelopes
– late and calling –
transliterated into oblivion.

red emissaries of the city
enter the evening on

tiptoes.

*Somnolence*

And the bird sheds its wings over the city,
and the white
         snows, feathers and petals
over the roofs and our
curtained faces
   naked windows.


The Kings have departed –
   across the backyard,
   forcing the locked gates of the city – ;
we have coined and counted
   all the stars,
and nailed them safe with our names
to their respective constellations.


The birdless wings cover and keep
white and warm
         our city.
In sleep, perfected with featherbeds,
we have outwitted the clocks.


A double windowpane
padded with mirrors
shields us from dust, ashes and time.

( As a counter-clockwise dawn comes
   to coincide
        with Lot's leaving).

*Apocalypse eve*
    *(of the sinners)*


And we walk on water
  with no purpose,
dispersed in all abolished directions.

and under the roofs stitched with needles
we rival with paper birds
               in the weaving of nests.

And we mark time wading in sand;
it retains no footprints, no foot, no time. –
and no mark is left of our passage.

And we wash the knowledge of our passage
off the cleanness of our spotless hands.

      There are mirrors buried in sand,
      in forests, in moonlight,
      in river water.

      And we walk up and down the river current,
      with our thoughts swimming in earth.

The clock has been broken and given
a new set of seven hours
sewn of one and the same
    reiterated minute.

And we walk in its light
and pace up its width. –

And stand and stand
  at the wide gate.

*Apocalypse eve*
           *(of the penitent)*


And the sky is raining its thirst.
And the fruits are ripe with names. And the stones.

And we live each bird's flight
as the sign of the Cross.

      And each wheel is freed from the circle.


We collect in cups and in cupped hands
the clouds' sap and the humid earth,
with seeds and bones
          sown as words

          from the skies' two hemispheres.


At the foot of the hill
there are known trees,
there are footpaths and kneepaths, up the hill.

There are stones. And shoulders

    for the lying of our heads.

We confess: we had been. – We offer unweighed
our treasure
of the space in-between.

*Apocalypse eve*
    *(of the just)*



And the fields are full,
and the chairs are set upright in the mid of the fields,
and the wheat is woven into the plaited white
locks. And the mills are milling water and wind.

We are anointed with a full sunshine,
                              in our waiting.
Sleepless and free from going back
in years, in clutches, in homes, in beauty.

And occupy an immovable place.

The sky is moonlightless, moonless, and sheds no dark.
The ravens are counted off;
and all birds are white, and are
the effaced messages.

At the kneeling seacoast we lay
our thankfulness as a supper,
and break
        the bread of each word.
Every broken pronoun –
        a chapel.

We compose a cradle, of our hands;
of our voices, a silence chalice.

Weightless, we kiss and erase
our fingerprints from the sand.

( The sackcloth we have worn
 is burnt with our ardour, –
 and so, too, is ashes ).

# *Alembics*

This poem reflects some of the main themes of the Christian ascetic spirituality. To be more precise, it deals with the beginning of this spiritual itinerary: the process of one's inner purification. Each part of the poem corresponds to a step one makes – or a *phase* one enters.

I wrote as I lived it.

The symbolism of the elements of water and fire – the two alembics – apart from a natural association with cleansing and purifying – allude to the words of St. John about baptism with water and with fire (*cf.* Matthew 3:11). Thus, *water* also means death-and-rebirth; here it corresponds to the first step of the purification – that of the senses. *Fire* refers to the second step – purification of the heart. In the biblical context, *fire* is Spirit, and Love.

It is worth noting that here *fire* appears only in the last two parts of the poem. To be purified by Love, is to become love. And since in this life one can hardly achieve the perfection of love, this poem shall always remain unfinished. And so it shall be a life-long poem, continually to be lived and written.

## 1.

   It is water that drowns our faces
     leaving the sole ultimate face
        upon the shore.
Invisible bird retraces the line of valleys and hills
and teaches us to acknowledge
  and know by heart
    its features.

Our words converge and become eyes,
our sunrises meet and become vision.

our soundless bows coincide, –
            a vertical path, a breath homewards.

                  We sculpt in bas-relief
                  a plane surface of our minds.


Upon the water we paint a sky,
        a cloth soaked in transparent pigment.
From the ebb and tide we learn and receive:
        a tabula rasa, *carte blanche* of a gift.

## 2.

When the water subsides
the drowning words and days
spread their garments upon the sand,
their thin sound and bodies
         lie with arms
splayed sunwards.

The Sunday rays dry and seam over
                      all folds.

their hands write on the sand
forgiveness
within the drawn circles.

Stones yield to oil with their
liquid chalcedony matter
    and grow a heart.

birds of the air migrate
  beyond the linear time
to its obverse surface.

## 3.

It is water that waits for our coming
across the current of counter-waters,
waits and empties
          our half-full glasses
cleansed of poison and of
the half-
      knowledge of poison.

it waits and places them on the edge of the border
and fills them half with a measure
of our own smallness.

The empty half evolves into space,
acquires depth, develops lungs. Exposed to the sun
it fills up
with a limpid solar forbearance.


It is water that
whitewashes the current,
grows bridges and fords
and viatical fishes,

it reaches out with its
still waters
         beyond our ebb and tide.

It is
    it
that proceeds
from its own mouth
and offers straits
and tightrope bridges

and waits for our coming over –
for our overcoming.

## 4.

We thank ice
for having remained
condemnation, transparent to light,
to word.    ( A faithful stasis
of walking in circles, up and down,
> the under-ladder ).

For having preserved the heat frozen,
safe in uncut hands of offence.
For having subsisted until
the vernal
      entering water
      as thaw water.

## 5.

Water speaks its agile immobility
           through the wing of a dragonfly,
bares knee-level the question
we pass silent over the ford.
           Water responds with a noon pendulum,
           with apostolic circles
           drawn on water,
           with fishes dispersed
           in all-embracing directions,
           carrying one symbol of one word.

We build a raft of the suncircles,
of our broken self-ful partitions,
of tails we set for vanes, fishwards,
the remnants of the absolved material.

           The day grants us the hour,
           a passage counter-clockwise.

           Water drowns the raft and teaches
           our feet linear walking.

## 6.

The soliloquy of the water
is our morning song.
                  A canticle
for the narrow path it has traced
between
vapour and ice.

            Words of the water dilute
            the solid property of the pronouns,
            weather out the commas,
                      semi-colons and thorns,
            alliterate our names, erode the consonants,
            quench the vowels.
                  Evaporate the brine;
                  extract their own salt.

For the unspeakable water tongues
we fold receptacles
of paper and porcelain,
store away in the air crates
the marionettes
      of our thoughts,
(the authorship
of our language).

Boats and ropes are denounced by water.
Our hands are shaped
by their synchronous lying still.

Drowned and saved and laid spread
on the inflammable side of the shore,
> water-reborn
> we pass on
> to the ordeal by fire.

## 7.

Fire foreknows the inflammable organs
of seeing, of reading the inner voices
that water will have
known and drowned
      and filled with vision, with hearing.

Flames make disappear the ladder's
lowest rungs
consummated in water.

For fear of salt
one doesn't look back.

Fire's language is hands of feathers,
hands cauterizing the wounds of colour,
of shape, of mis-knowledge, the swells of senses,
the calluses of the flat three-dimensional spaces.

The tongue of fire is meta-language.

Spoken through,
      we are meta-named
into a non-flammable species.

*( interlude )*

Trees are called upon by
the alembic elements
    to be their bridges, witnesses, ballasts.
        We call on the trees to be our
        mirrors, canes, chaperons,
        our all-embracing antecedents.

We rehearse an à priori obedience,
nestle with birds and sunlight
in the woven projections
        of future and past.

Leaves and branches inscribe
our names among the rings
of their arboreal tablets.

## 8.

Fire chooses the front door,
a damp season, masonry days
      soothed in fatigue,
makes itself felt in loosed knots,
in knotless moorings,
in light dispensed of the flames.

Fire allies with the foresight,
denounces all coincidences,
replaces all reason with one
      single non-cerebral thought,
immobilises the scales of all ratios.

It is fire that flies in a bird's wing,
weaves nests, breaks shells,
burns out: archives, mise-en-scènes, ambivalence.

(Fire takes on a lavender colour,
dissimulates its name
behind the lavender scent,
makes itself recognisable
by a handful of ashes it carries
      in its ever-full hands).

Fire greets us with faith and doubts,
holds us a mirror, breaks it into splinters.

Shapes us a new face,
cauterises our human features.

    We examine the burns' symmetrical patterns,
    byzantine ornaments, indelible depth.

    From the fire we learn
    our name
            as a password.

## 9.

Sunday: estuary
of water, of fire, of tree sap,

of liquid mountain crests,
of wheat rivers.

It comes barefoot, carrying baskets of sunlight:
three measures of day
to seven measures of time.

A limpid finger writes on the wall
the yellow words of its teaching.


We walk into Sunday on yellow ropes.
Knee-level, we are
saved and drowned.

# Part 2

*« And immediately they left their nets »*
*( Matthew 4:20 )*

## Spring Canticle

When the snow subsides
beyond its *raison d'être*,
mills are milling a new flour

the flight of birds,
stripped of its off-white background,
twines with the all-embracing sky
the naked line of the horizon.

The thaw water, pure and delivered,
carries its pearls
of lessness and fullness.
        Orphancy sprouts.   We sit on the porch,
        our eyes welling with sunlight.

## A Song for Elias

Water well     sun well
prophetic resistance
to stone and arrow
      to tongues
         of fire
distilling the souls upwards
to heaven via
aqueducts, logs, bows.

The chariot built
    in a simple syntactic order.
The chant, of a circular verbal matter.

Prophets sow themselves into the ploughed soil,
and burn forth
in heartfuls    in handfuls.

If in the heart I find no water –
                              and no thirst,
no swinging movements of no branches
answerable to the wind of the South;

and no arid sand   secure sand,
  no sand of the quick or dead
          no quicksand,

if in the heart I hear no voices
directed parallel to the horizon,
no verbal splinters that cut the cords
     and slip in-between the heart's systoles,

if in the heart I read no symbols
of no self-referral semiosis,
      no over-thought, no arrogated being,
      no ripe and pitted fruit of the Garden.

If in the heart I feel no future:
no temporality,
         neither nadir nor zenith,

              no open doors, no antechambers
              leading
              into the furnished rooms'

    circular enfilades
    ever-empty, –


Then the earth of my heart
has been ploughed with anchors; –
      and laid
      fallow
over fertile winters.

Then the seed in my heart
has become a sprout,
the pace of my heart –
   an unrocking cradle;
the life of its fruit – a sleepless Garden,
its kernel – the ever-consuming,
   and ever-consumed
     flame.

*Epiphany*

We bring in the crates the sawdust
the shavings and speech of the trees who had been
our chaperones, who would have been
our table- and bed-steads – and were
the timber whereof we have built
our boats and rafts.

We bring and lay in the open chests
the treasure of our white pages:
erased *able*s, *willing*s and *ready*s, –
blank sheets lined by the day;
   small pearls of the virgin hours
   stripped of the heritage
   of the stencils;
bread pellets, ancestral guilt
inscribed upon our fingers –
      ( the penance whereof we bake
  our daily bread ).

In the treasure of our open chests
we bring a doorless and cornerless chamber, –
a handful of stones from the walls,
  whereof
the wisdom our words
was bleached, bleached
          and erased.

We have seen and followed
the ultimate star: we have travelled light
                                    and barefoot, one way.

We wait for the Kings to depart,
and kneel and wash
the feet of the Shepherds.

A mine glass empty with water,
pure with sediment's reminiscence,
with their sedi-
 mental affliction
absolved in the salt
of the sea water.

the glass, mine with obliteration
of the capital letters;
with water
cleansed from the sparkling,
pure and still with a mute recollection.

a vitric transparency
 to the sun.
Raindrops, absorbed and departed
in vapour.
a selfless invisible green sprout
born from the ever-fertile
emptiness.

 (nothing drowns,
  nor stays on the surface
  within the plenitude empty to eyes:

the firm and the brittle, united
in the unspillability
        of the content)

This tree, departed from its species,
  all ashes sweeper.

in our secret, we grow
    skin and bark,
    root-less/-full,
  *sacri-* and *sancti-*
      -fied
kernels and bones,
  sky- and heaven-
      wards.


( We part and depart,
  abnegate and negate
    ourselves,
     taking turns,
in the deciduous season,
   season of florescence,
dispelling our selves,
spelling
     the selves away,
upholding each other – for bridges –
slenderly, over each winter )

in our secret
we are in light:
a spacious room,
a timeless hour.

Here, you have grown an olive branch.
Here, I am seeing the dove in.

ink and paper
cross and plough

                ripening fruits,
                *Vôtres*

*les miens*: arms
too light to fly
too light to sink
too blind to count
too open to carry
too bare
        to bear a name.

An illegitimate language,
                  *mine*,
discalced, orphan and hermit.

a daily ultimate sip
of thirst,
the Thebaid purpose
            and reflex.

A grain of sand
covering miles of legends.
A drop of water capsizing the Babel vessel.

Illegitimate language, –
a bridge and a walk
 over the circuits.

Each verbal unit
pronounced = denounced :

a narrow path
  towards Adoption.

## Mt 5:39

Supple and swift
          recurrent movement
of cheeks' taking turns
on behalf
of your inner chambers

the flapping curtains of your windows
settle in peace
without folds

a tear or two cleanse the pane,
a sunray begins its walk
from the sill.

A bird alights upon the respite
between the cheeks'
          last but one and the last turn,
to peck at the grains of corn
    from your smarting skin.

*from* **Pastoral cycle**

Lime-painted days
whitewashed in clouds'
          humid discretion.

There is grass.   Herbs' envy.

A simple walk hand in hand with a cane,
the light-footed heart pacing the space
free from the counter-clockwise time
        of recollection.

In the field and the poverty
there are seeds lost and found:
thrice homeful,
     pregnant with their fulfilment
     in bread and in dry bread.

The sunflowers, overgrown with life,
offer themselves
as subjective sundials.

Single-handed, the path overcomes
the other directions
     bleached and erased
     from the book of years.

The lost and found, sown along the path,
sings in the birds' canticle;
sprouts;
the cane blossoms.

*from* **Pastoral cycle**

Substitute for the ink and paper,
for the daily bread of their endeavour,
      with salutary raindrops
      and dry herbs
      equated with grass, freed from envy.

  Time is given and taken,
and reinstated in its well-tempered
                  finite quality.

                    Substitute with spirit
                    for inspiration;
        (blessed are the poor,
        the paths overgrown with clover).

With the ebb and tide
of the sunlight and clouds,
the ink subsides, leaving no flotsam,
   no stains, no commas, no points omitted.

Pages, awaiting, tempered with years' covenants,
perfect their white colour
    with the sun and the thought
    of a hay prospect.

Grass subsists, clings to the sky.

The path, walked, retains the footprints
and heals them over
        with silent bells, with the scent
of clover and poverty.

## *Autumnal*

*Helmutplatz* calls me
a shadow daughter,
holds to my lowered eyes
its fruits – the ash tree
      leafing day-night
      its sounds:
in the folds of our
   stillness and thought
we bear a prosody and
a botanical knowledge:

   we are silent
   expectant
   one-another-wards.


Eyelids and foliage
cradle the daylight,
shed the reflections and cover
our roots with secrets;
    bare,
      our arms and branches
      twine around an embryo season
        of our common florescence.

With kernels and bones of our fruits
we nurture the precious poverty

    of this unsalted
          unleavened autumn


and are inhabited,
taking turns,
by one another's reflections upon
the windows' deepest surface
   ( a home we have
 in common).

We reward with oblivion
    our selves,
    and are:
a diamondless crown and
an unsteered boat.


  On our feast days
we bow to ( and shed
leaves over )
  the ground.

## Ode to Spring

White councils
of the season

sun-bleached days
  before the harvest.

Rooms enfold with a static confidence
afternoon hours lived with windows'
immaculate lungs, umbilical sunlight.

An angel draws upon the wall
  words eternally pregnant with silence:

unspoken, with clasped hands,
we lean against his wings.

A newly reborn hour
bequeaths us its renatal clothes.
         We exit the clock and slough
         our names and shadows.

         The angel retraces upon the sky
             our outlines
             with chalk.

## *Fürbitte*

Franz Kafka once said that "writing is a form of prayer." Poetry – as an *essentialized* form of writing – allows a yet sharper focus: and a poem often *becomes* a prayer.

In the case of *'Fürbitte'*[1], however, it was a prayer that became a poem.

This cycle was born as an "offspring" of a special prayer I was asked to write for the day of my wedding, to be read during the ceremony in the church. Traditionally, it is a combination of blessings, of wishes and supplications to obtain certain graces for the couple. Thus it consists, as prayers often do, mainly in *asking*.

Yet I felt that one (and perhaps the most essential) part would be omitted: that of *offering,* of *giving*. Prayer, an elevation of the soul in its purest form, is a daughter of thankfulness – and of love. And love is to give love. And, simply, to give. This cycle of poems is less an echo of my reflections upon what I can give (for indeed what *can* I give…? and what do I *have?* and *"what do I have that I did not receive?"*), than a Canticle of a soul moved by this desire to give, to offer, to immolate: the little it has, the nothing it has, the very desire it has to give, and its very self.

The initial imperative *"Offer…"* wherewith the soul addresses itself, becomes at the end *"You are offered…"* – as a reminder of the graces received, and also as an evident equitation: giving is receiving. Giving oneself, ultimately – and receiving, ultimately, among other graces, one's true self.

---

[1] *Fürbitte* (German) – a prayer to God, as an intercession on behalf of another.

Offer fingerbones to the Lord:
knuckles' idio-
-syncratic symmetry,
gossamer skin enlaced with His given
of years' eternal bound content.


a non-movement a non-utterance
dwell around the bones
of your fingers; the northern wind comes to talk
through your shoulders, and coats your shoulderbones with
       His shielding.


The Lord hears the length of your skin,
the woollen gaze at a dawn window.
The voice is your spouse. The fog's words
descend to inhabit the palm of the street,
at the eternally bound
received and offered
  hour
     of this morning.

Offer the Lord   bloodless and dry
lips on the wind,
their silent walk
         close to the pavement:
immolation of their
spoken being, scars
  on your Lenten poetry,

  a black-and-white stucco
  enclosed in time.

Offer the porch,
the uncounted steps
around the precipice
            of exemptions.

Offer water reborn in water.
Your kneading and still fingers,
bound for bread and unabridged
    hours of the evening.

The mist over the rooftops
you receive for a soul cover.

Your morning pilgrimage
                    sunwards
   is but the length of the street.

Offer on the instalment plan
the uncovered unbleached
whiteness and silence

of the bones
        of your fingers, –
a cloth laid in between the days
of wakeless- and wakeful-
        -ness.

Offer an hourpath at dawn
your eyes have accomplished
                upon the pane,
the black leaves, chaperones of your lips,
and
every word steeped in ink.

    Offer yourself
    as a home
    for the heavy invisible Anchor.

Offer the Lord an ivory-green
tower of abandonment. The bell chimes and days
pasted back, sewn together with One will.

Offer your will – in return for wax.

(offer candles that grow
			into being,
through growing smaller,
through their innocence).

		Offer each word whereof
		you have erased the sound.

A letter, century-late, will amend
your voice,
will teach it to learn
		its centripetal course, –
		from Lent to Lent
			to grow down.

The vernal sap, a solvent ointment,
sleeps on your fingertips
			lulled with awaiting,
			unceasing and glove-like
			like that of ivy.

Offer
an ivory-green monobeing, –

                                to the sole skylight.


Offer the tower.

Offer the Lord:   space
                    a spoonful of days
                suspended midair,

fingers' stillness
folding upon itself.

            You listen inward
                    into being one
                    of the silent diaphanous beings.

A thawing light
offers your eyes
        the *woulds*'
evergreen fruit. –

The sunlight beyond your eyelids
knows the mellow,
the ripe, the sole
        answer's kernel.



            ( in the hands of the Sower
            your fingers' stillness – is
            the field and the plough).

On a summit day, offer the Lord
the yield
       of your sole fruit harvest:
      a bitter-sweet sleepless seed
      loosed from its astringent core.

Offer the Lord the bottomless nothing
of *can* and of *do*
of your faithful hand. Offer the clean space
                                      of your *may*,
the muted sound of all utterance.

Fill with a virgin earth
your empty cup brimful of water, –

    validate in fire
        your white clay.

Offer the scaffoldings
of your house:
ribs' and chestbones'
spacious chambers,
skin-curtains' transparent fabric,
thick walls
    of the foveal sight.

( All windowpanes
  are absolved from the crows;
  All staircases – from the out-of-breath.

      It is a time of gold and mended sleeves ).

Offer your oil lamp
and your green
sun-impregnated eyes,

their common light –
   on the last
    feast day
  of your shutters.

You are offered a rain
    selected among the clouds of mind'
      circular movements,
   among the arid aestival straits
   crossed walking upon the ropes,
   and boats nailed to the builders' hand,
   and draughts'
   vectorless birds of prey.

in the rain you are offered:
    selected water, re-natal, erosive
      for sound and faces.

( Your pockets are full of migrating birds,
  of virgin paper, of ink
   foreknown in its
    divine
   configuration. )

You are offered a jasmine-scented
                cessation of sounds,
a vision at an oblique angle of nameless
        and timeless days' essence,

a touch of a meta-material porcelain,
a curtain over the seen
        upholstery of the courtyard.


You are offered to drink from a liquid sunlight,
the black leaves'
        verbal incisions, verbal bandages.

You see the clouds descend in the form of clouds,
the clock halt to develop
        a fourth pointer.

You are offered a wing
           of your left hand's
    emptiness,
    loosed strings,
    desireless surface.

You receive the offer with your
    rightwinged hand.

The daylight breathes through your lungs,
conductive of oxygen.

The name of the offering rests on your shoulders
    unburdened of all
    hide-and-seek names.

The straight line of your spine,
    your walking cane ever in blossom.


With the sun on your back and face
you stand in your own zenith. –

        The shadow-pointer under your feet
        shows the way.

# Notes

Part I

*"arid alluvial / wrong and vital…"*
for an ampler understanding of this piece, see the poem *'Paris (porte-à-faux)',* included in my previous collection, *Antibodies*, which begins *"arid alluvial wrong city…"*

Let the words *'left'* and *'right'* have multiple meaning:
*'right'* as the opposite of *'left'* as well as the opposite of *'wrong'*; living in Paris I used to take daily walks crossing the Seine and going from the Left Bank to the Right Bank of the city, thus "connecting" them in me; the word *'left'*, especially as the French language has it ("gauche"), has also the sense of *'white crow'* or *'black sheep'*.

*"Winter prevails…"*
both pieces echo poems from a sequence that start *"Sadness prevails…",* included in my previous collection *Antibodies*; the crows here also would be the same ones.

*Lisieux* and *Schauflergasse* refer, respectively, to the Carmelite monastery of Lisieux (at the time I was working on this poem I was also reading the *Letters* of St. Thérèse of Lisieux; the Carmelite Order is one of the most austere monastic orders); and to a street that I had before me every day, a street in Vienna, adjacent to Hofburg with all its exuberance, riches and splendour.

*from Wandering cycles –*
the first line, *"And eat our bread at the face of the window…",* is taken from one of the *"Winter prevails…"*

*Apocalypse eve (of the penitent) –*
"In the last verse, a short explanation is perhaps needed : *"the space in-between"* is the space of time elapsed between "we had been" (in past perfect) and "we confess" (in present), i.e. the time which would be thus in present perfect – the time of penitence spent between the 'had *been*' (in all the sense of our sinful human way of being), as the now, the last day before the Apocalypse.

*"Alembics"*:
*"forgiveness / within the drawn circles"*: an image alluding vaguely to a scene in the Gospel of St. John (8:7). Somehow I always imagine that it was *circles* that Jesus was drawing on the ground.

*"birds of the air"*:
cf. Matthew 13:32

*"apostolic circles / drawn on water"* can be understood as the same kind of circles mentioned in the note above, with the lines that follow immediately alluding to the dispersion of the Apostles.

ordeal by fire:
a medieval trial in which, to prove his innocence, the accused had to walk a certain distance over red-hot ploughshares or to hold a red-hot iron rod; if he were innocent, he was supposed to remain unscathed.

*"for fear of salt / one doesn't look back"*:
allusion to Lot's wife who, having looked back while fleeing Sodom, became a pillar of salt (Genesis 19:26)


Part 2

*"This tree departed from its species…"* –
The olive branch and the dove allude to the Biblical deluge, Noah's Ark having already appeared in the Part 1 (see the poem *"to restore the outer edge…"* from *Wandering cycles*)

*"ink and paper / cross and plough…"* –
The Thebaid desert was a place of settlement of the first Christian anchorites, and the beginning of the ascetic mysticism.

*from Pastoral cycle* –
The blossoming cane, which also appears in the last poem of the cycle 'Fürbitte', stands simply for a miracle (as in The Old Testament): a *miracle* the origin of which is known, is the opposite of the *miraculous*.

www.ingramcontent.com/pod-product-compliance
Lightning Source LLC
Chambersburg PA
CBHW030908170426
43193CB00009BA/774